ARE YOU A

CHRISTIAN?

[OR ARE YOU DECEIVED]

TORBEN SØNDERGAARD

ARE YOU A
CHRISTIAN?
[OR ARE YOU DECEIVED]

By Torben Søndergaard

The Laurus Company, Inc. ISBN: 978-1-943523-87-0

PUBLISHED BY THE LAST REFORMATION
IN ASSOCIATION WITH THE LAURUS COMPANY, INC.
PUBLISHED IN THE UNITED STATES OF AMERICA

This book may be purchased in paperback from
TheLastReformation.com, Amazon.com, and other retailers
around the world.
Available in Spring Arbor for retailers.

Introduction

I was born in 1976 and grew up in an ordinary Danish family. We were members of the state church, as are most people in Denmark.

As was normal for the state church, I was baptized as an infant and confirmed later. Like the majority of people in Denmark, we never actually went to church. I had never read the Bible and rarely prayed to God. Still, I considered myself a Christian since I was both baptized and confirmed by the church. I thought I had done what Christianity required, and if I died, I would go to heaven as the priest had promised me. But, oh, was I wrong!

One day while visiting a good friend, I got a shock. There on his bed was a Bible. My first thought was, "What is he doing with a Bible? It is for old people who have nothing else to do." To my great surprise, he told me that he had just become a Christian and had experienced God.

When I heard this, I thought he had gone mad. So I told him he was crazy and brainwashed because you could not "experience" God.

To me, Christianity was all about having a blind belief in "something" out there somewhere and to love your neighbor as yourself, but the more he told me, the more surprised I was. Christianity was not what I thought!

A few days later, I repented and turned to God. I met Him in a radical way! I experienced something like a mighty fire going through my whole body. It is hard to describe. It was so real, and I still remember it as if it happened yesterday. Since that day, April 5th, 1995, at 9:30 p.m., incredible things have happened in my life.

The fear of dying and depression, with which I had sometimes struggled, had gone. Instead, I had joy, peace, and freedom that I had never experienced before. And the biggest thing was that God was now a reality in my life.

Before, when I had tried to pray to God, I experienced nothing. It was as if there was a wall between Him and me, as if God was not there at all. This is quite different today.

Today, I know that He is near. He speaks to me and hears my prayers. For example, a few months after I became a Christian, I was at a concert in Aalborg, Denmark, and suddenly, God spoke to me clearly. He said: "Torben, the girl standing behind you will be your wife one day." I turned around, and six or seven rows back, I saw a girl in an orange dress, and I knew it was her. When the concert was over, I had to drive home with a friend, so I only managed to smile at her.

In the car on my way home, I said to my friend, "Michael, I have just met my future wife. I do not know her name, her age, or where she comes from, but God has said that the girl in the orange dress will one day be my wife."

When I got home, I asked God to bring us together. I did not know where she was from or anything about her, but I knew God had everything under control, just like everything else.

Three months after first seeing her at the concert, He brought us together. Now we have been married for 20 years, and we have three beautiful children.

This is just one of hundreds of examples I could share of how God speaks, leads, and makes the impossible possible. I have also seen thousands of people healed when I prayed for them. I have seen many people set free from demons.

I have received dreams and visions from God that have become a reality. Yes, I have experienced the same life that the first Christians experienced in the New Testament book of Acts, a supernatural life where the Holy Spirit leads on a daily basis.

Today, I travel the world and tell others about Jesus and then see them experience the same things I experience. I have also written several books, published in seven different languages. I have a YouTube channel with millions of views and an online Bible school that has taught over a hundred thousand worldwide.

None of this is because I am skilled or special. My life before God entered it was actually very boring and average. This is just a little part of my journey with God that started on 5 April 1995. Yours can start today! God can transform your life as He has transformed mine. It can happen through this ooklet that will tell you how to get born again and xperience God in a new way.

— Torben Søndergaard

Are You A Christian?

The booklet was originally written because many people in Western countries call themselves Christians but have a completely wrong idea of what it means to be a Christian. Many know and learn about "Christianity" as a religion, but few know of the personal, supernatural life with God that you can read about in the Bible.

You might live in a country where many priests do not even know God. So when the priests, Sunday after Sunday, preach or make statements in the media about Christianity, they often present a distorted picture of what a Christian is. They are blind leaders of the blind, as Jesus says:

> *"Let them alone. They* [priests and religious leaders] *are blind leaders of the blind. And if the blind leads the blind, both will fall into a ditch."*
> — MATTHEW 15:14 (NKJV)

The purpose of this small booklet, is to show you what the Holy Bible says about being a Christian. Throughout this booklet, you will find quotations from the Bible that show the truth of what it says.

Allow me to tell you that if you are reading this booklet in order to find out whether you are a Christian or not, then you are not because being a Christian means you have accepted the forgiveness of Jesus and have been "born again." This is something that happens inside of you. It is something so real and supernatural that you are not in doubt.

The Holy Spirit opens your spiritual eyes so you can know God. He confirms to you that you have become a child of God:

> For you did not receive the spirit of bondage again to fear, but you received the Spirit of adoption by whom we cry out, "Abba, Father." The Spirit Himself bears witness with our spirit that we are children of God."
>
> — ROMANS 8:15-16 (NKJV)

When you are born again, you begin to understand who God is, and you start to see the kingdom of God:

> Jesus answered and said unto him, Verily, verily, I say unto thee, Except a man be born again, he cannot see the kingdom of God.
>
> — JOHN 3:3 (KJV)

9

Calling yourself a Christian does not make you a Christian. It cannot make you a Christian. Exactly like calling yourself a car cannot make you a car. You cannot become a Christian by being baptized as an infant and later being confirmed, or by going to church occasionally. It is a matter of becoming a new creature through rebirth.

When this happens, you are made new on the inside, and you have a new life in Christ that can be seen externally, a wonderful new life where God is with you. It is a life where the Holy Spirit leads and guides you so that your life looks like what we read in the Bible:

> *Therefore if any man be in Christ, he is a new creature: old things are passed away; behold, all things are become new.*
> — 2 CORINTHIANS 5:17 (KJV)

When you become a new creature, you know it!

I do not doubt whether I am married or not. I clearly remember the day and date we were married. We live together, eat together, sleep together, and we ven have three children together. The same way, I do not doubt whether I am a Christian or not because I live with God. I have fellowship with Him, talk to Him, and get to know Him better each day.

If you are unsure whether you are a Christian or not, then you are not. If you are unsure if you know Him and live with Him, you can become sure today and get to know Him.

What is a Christian?

The word "Christian," comes from the word "Christos," meaning "little Christ." "Christian" was actually not a word that Jesus used.

Neither did the first "Christians." It was not until 13 years after Jesus was crucified that they began to use the word. Up to that time, they used the word "disciple," a disciple of Jesus.

The first disciples followed Jesus and learned from Him. They came to be like Him more and more in their words and actions. They looked like Jesus so much that people began to call them "Christian" as a nickname. Note that it was others who began to call them Christians because it was evident to everyone that they lived with Jesus. It was not because they lived in a "Christian" country, went to church on Sunday, were baptized as babies, and were confirmed in the church.

... And the disciples were called Christians first in Antioch.
— ACTS 11:26 (KJV)

A Christian is, therefore, a disciple of Christ. But what is a disciple?

The word "disciple" (translated from the Greek "matheteuo") has a certain meaning. It means "to be a disciple of one. You follow his regulations, rules, teachings, instructions and orders, as a student or trainee."

A disciple of Jesus is, therefore, a follower, a pupil, an apprentice. They were apprentices of Jesus with the goal of eventually becoming like their master:

> The disciple [apprentice] is not above his master: but every one that is perfect shall be as his master.
> — LUKE 6:40 (KJV)

Jesus' command to His disciples before He ascended to heaven, was that they were to make all nations His disciples and teach them to do everything He had commanded:

> Go ye therefore, and teach all nations, baptizing them ... Teaching them to observe all things whatsoever I have commanded you: and, lo, I am with you always, even unto the end of the world.
> — MATTHEW 28:19-20 (KJV)

His command was not that they should create religious people—people who do not know Him nor obey His commands, but still call themselves Christians.

If people understood this today, many would not be so quick to say they are "Christians." Being a Christian involves much more than just going to church once a week or living a good life. It means to follow Jesus and learn to keep what He has commanded us.

I don't become a policeman just by calling myself a "policeman." I need to be trained to obey the authority I am under. Likewise, it makes no difference whether you call yourself a Christian or not. If you are not a disciple of Jesus who keeps His commandments, you will still be on your way to damnation.

Many Are Deceived

Some time ago, I was in the city talking with a lady in her mid-fifties. She was sure that she was a Christian. She told me that she and the Lord had made an agreement and that He was there for her if she needed Him. She thought that because she was baptized, confirmed, and went to church occasionally, He would take her to heaven when she died.

I could easily discern, however, that the god she believed in was a god she had created in her own fantasy. It was a god that suited her and not the true and living God that the Bible talks about, the God who created us all and wants fellowship with us through His Son, Jesus Christ.

So I asked her if she knew Jesus. I explained to her that if you know Jesus, you must also keep His commandments.

> *"The one who says "I have come to know God" and yet does not keep his commandments is a liar, and the truth is not in such a person.*
> — 1 John 2:4 (NET)

I asked her if she really knew what His commandments are. She had to admit that she did not know much about Jesus or about keeping His commandments.

She said that she believed in God, and she believed that she would go to heaven when she died because she had been living as a good person.

I said to her, which I can unfortunately say to many "Christians," that she did not know God. The god she believed in was not the God who had created her and who can save her. It was her own little imaginary idol, a god that fits her needs, a god who has no expectations of her.

The truth is that she had created an idol that cannot save her on the day of judgment, although she secretly hoped it would.

I also explained to her that, in our own power, we cannot live up to God's standard. Therefore, we should not compare ourselves to an addict or a mass murderer. The truth is that we all have sinned and have broken God's Law and therefore need forgiveness, a forgiveness that can be found only in Jesus. I told her that if she did not repent and

urn to God—the one true God, the God of the
Bible, and the One who created the whole universe
—and be born again, being baptized into Jesus,
and receiving the Holy Spirit, she would, as the
Bible says, perish forever.

What Characterizes a Christian?

Several times, when I have been at a funeral and talked with the relatives about God, heaven, and hell, they often say that the deceased believed in God. They will say that the person was not the type to talk about it, nor was fanatical, but believed in his own way deep inside.

One of the characteristics of a Christian is that you have an active faith. Faith must lead to repentance, then to baptism, and so on. The Bible makes it clear that faith without works is dead. Faith without action is dead, and a faith that cannot be seen is not true faith:

> But someone will say, "You have faith; I have deeds." Show me your faith without deeds, and I will show you my faith by my deeds. You believe that there is one God. Good! Even the demons believe that—and shudder. … As the body without the spirit is dead, so faith without deeds is dead.
> — JAMES 2:18-19, 26 (NIV)

The first thing faith will cause you to do is to repent and turn to God.

This makes you stop living in sin as you did before you came to believe in Christ. It will show that you really are a Christian and know Jesus.

> *No one who is born of God will continue to sin, because God's seed remains in them; they cannot go on sinning, because they have been born of God. This is how we know who the children of God are and who the children of the devil are: ...*
> — 1 JOHN 3:9-10A (NIV)

Another characteristic of being a Christian is that you talk about Jesus. You cannot help but talk about Him because you are so full of Him and everything He has done:

> *The good person out of the good treasury of his heart produces good, and the evil person out of his evil treasury produces evil, for his mouth speaks from what fills his heart."*
> — LUKE 6:45 (NET)

When we are full of Jesus, we will tell others about Him. You cannot be a Christian without the people around you hearing about it. Jesus is also radical in this way:

> *Whosoever therefore shall confess me before men*
> *him will I confess also before my Father which is*
> *in heaven. But whosoever shall deny me before*
> *men, him will I also deny before my Father which*
> *is in heaven.*
> — MATTHEW 10:32-33 (KJV)

Jesus also says that supernatural signs will follow those who believe in Him:

> *And these signs shall follow them that believe; In*
> *my name shall they cast out devils; they shall*
> *speak with new tongues; ... they shall lay hands*
> *on the sick, and they shall recover.*
> — MARK 16:17-18 (KJV)

The word "sign" has the same meaning as a sign that you put outside a store. The sign shows what is for sale inside the store. If there is a sign with a picture of bread hanging outside the store, then you know it is a bakery and that you can get bread inside the store. Similarly, what characterizes a true Christian (a disciple) is speaking in tongues, casting out demons, and laying hands on the sick. Being a Christian is to live a supernatural life. It

s a life where the Holy Spirit speaks and leads,
where you speak in tongues, heal the sick, and
cast out demons.

Baptism in Water and The Holy Spirit

It may sound like a burden to obey Jesus. But when you experience the new birth, get baptized, and receive the Holy Spirit within you, everything becomes different. An important part of being a Christian and a follower of Jesus is the baptism in water and in the Spirit, for it is by the baptism where you bury the old life, and by the Holy Spirit that you get the real desire inside you to obey Jesus. Yes, without the Holy Spirit, you cannot live the life God wants for you. Jesus Himself says this

> *"Come to Me, all you who are weary and burdened, and I will give you rest. Take my yoke on you and learn from me, because I am gentle and humble in heart, and you will find rest for your souls. For my yoke is easy to bear, and my load is not hard to carry."*
> — MATTHEW 11:28-30 (NET)

I know of several people who had gone to church

or many years. One day, they were baptized on their own faith and with the Holy Spirit, and then everything changed. Their relationship with God was suddenly much more alive.

They experienced a completely new perspective on life and saw things as they never had before. Yes, they had strength to live a life like they read about in the Bible.

Unfortunately, many believe they receive the Holy Spirit in baptism and then stop there. Even John the Baptist said that he only baptized in water and that Jesus would baptize with the Holy Spirit:

> "I [John] *baptize you with water, for repentance, but the one* [Jesus] *coming after me is more powerful than I am—I am not worthy to carry his sandals! He will baptize you with the Holy Spirit and fire.*"
> — MATTHEW 3:11 (NET)

When we talk about baptism in the Spirit, I must clarify that this is not something that happens when babies are baptized in the name of the Father, Son, and Holy Spirit in a church. Even if you have been told that you have received the Holy Spirit at that point, it's not true. When the Holy Spirit comes, everything becomes different. In the Bible they never baptized infants. Baptism was always on your own faith, by full immersion.

When Jesus walked on earth, He was with His disciples day in and day out for three years. He taught them, answered their questions, and encouraged them when it was hard, and they saw Him do great signs and wonders. It must have been amazing to be with Jesus. Still, Jesus told His disciples that it was best for them that He should go away, for if He did not go away, He could not send the Holy Spirit to them:

> *But very truly I tell you, it is for your good that I am going away. Unless I go away, the Advocate [The Holy Spirit] will not come to you; but if I go, I will send him to you.*
> — JOHN 16:7 (NIV)

When you are baptized in the Holy Spirit, the Holy Spirit helps you to live a life that pleases God. He will remind you of all that Jesus said, and He gives you power so that you can bear witness of Jesus:

> *But you will receive power when the Holy Spirit*

has come upon you, and you will be my witnesses in Jerusalem, and in all Judea and Samaria, and to the farthest parts of the earth.
— ACTS 1:8 (NET)

We have power when the Holy Spirit comes upon us and in us. Yet, it is not just the power to tell others about God with words, but it is also the power to heal the sick, set people free from demons, to prophesy, and to do much more. Yes, it is power to live a life like the one we read about in the Book of Acts in the Bible, a supernatural life led by the Holy Spirit.

In the baptism in water, you bury the old life, and in the baptism in the Holy Spirit, you receive power to live out the new life.

Baptism in Water

Many denominations in many countries still practice infant baptism. Infant baptism is not a biblical thing. The word "baptism" (in Greek "*baptizo*") means full immersion. This word is used to describe something or someone who is submerged under water, like in the old days when people would color or dye cloth. When the fabric was colored by being put under water, it had been baptized.

Baptism in water, as we see in the Bible, is submersion under water. It is only done after you have believed and acknowledged that you have sinned against God. When you recognize that you have sinned, then you can be washed clean:

> *And now why are you waiting? Arise and be baptized, and wash away your sins, calling on the name of the Lord.*
> — Acts 22:16 (NKJV)

There is something really wonderful about baptism. We have seen so many people set free and receive a whole new life when they were baptized.

eople often cry tears of joy, and demons lose their rip on people as soon as they come out of the vater. Yes, baptism is much more than just a symbol. The biblical baptism into Jesus is something upernatural that washes away all sin and shame. Then you arise to a new life!

> *Or don't you know that all of us who were baptized [fully immersed] into Christ Jesus were baptized into his death? We were therefore buried with him through baptism into death in order that, just as Christ was raised from the dead through the glory of the Father, we too may live a new life.*
> — ROMANS 6:3-5 (NIV)

Repentance, baptism in water, and the Holy Spirit

Many have a belief in a higher power but do not see themselves as a sinner in need of forgiveness.

However, when Jesus walked the earth, He preached repentance and turning to God:

From that time Jesus began to preach and to say,
"Repent, for the kingdom of heaven is at hand."
— MATTHEW 4:17 (NKJV)

Later, Jesus spoke of how one must be born again
by being baptized in water and the Holy Spirit:

Jesus answered, "I tell you the solemn truth, unless
a person is born of water and spirit, he cannot
enter the kingdom of God. What is born of the
flesh is flesh, and what is born of the Spirit is spirit."
— JOHN 3:5-6 (NET)

Before this could happen, Jesus had to die on the
cross for our sins. After His resurrection, He went
up to Heaven and sent the Holy Spirit down to
Earth. When this happened, the new covenant was
complete, and people could experience the Kingdom of God by turning to God, being baptized in
water, receiving forgiveness of sins, and then receiving the Holy Spirit. Therefore, when the first Christians preached the gospel of Jesus, they said this:

Then Peter said unto them, Repent, and be bap-
tized every one of you in the name of Jesus Christ
for the remission of sins, and ye shall receive the
gift of the Holy Spirit. For the promise is unto you,

and to your children, and to all that are afar off,
even as many as the Lord our God shall call.
— ACTS 2:38-39 (KJV)

The Bible says that there is only salvation through
faith in Jesus. It is not enough to believe in Jesus
as a historical figure who once lived.

When the Bible says that faith in Jesus saves,
it means to believe in Him and what He says:

"As He spoke these words, many believed in Him."
— JOHN 8:30 (NKJV)

And what did they come to believe? Did they only
come to believe that Jesus was a real person? No,
they came to believe that what He said was true!

Some years ago, I tried a bungee jump. I stood on
a platform 55 meters high. Before I could jump off,
I had to believe that the rubber band would hold
me and that it was not too long either. When I was
about to jump, I had faith and firm confidence that
it would go well. Because if it did not, well, then I
would die! If faith was not there, I would not have
jumped. It would have been really stupid!

If we replaced the rubber band with faith in Jesus,

would you jump? Are you willing to bet your life on what you believe? Even if it means you will be persecuted, bullied, and it might even cost you your life? Do you want to be baptized into Jesus even though others do not understand it?

Do you want to receive it or reject it?

How Do You Get the Holy Spirit?

Every week, we see people being baptized with the Holy Spirit. This often occurs in connection with water baptism. Once people have repented and have been baptized on their own faith, we then lay hands on them and pray. Often the Holy Spirit comes over them after a few minutes, and they begin to speak in tongues, just like we read about in the Bible.

> So Paul asked, "Then what baptism did you receive?" "John's baptism," they replied. Paul said, "John's baptism was a baptism of repentance. He told the people to believe in the one coming after him, that is, in Jesus." On hearing this, they were baptized in the name of the Lord Jesus. When Paul placed his hands on them, the Holy Spirit came on them, and they spoke in tongues and prophesied."
> — ACTS 19:3-6 (NIV)

Speaking in tongues means speaking in a divine

language. It is a language received by those who know God when they are baptized with the Holy Spirit. It is a language that you do not understand, but where your spirit prays to God and intercedes, builds up, worships, and much more:

> *For the one speaking in a tongue does not speak to people but to God, for no one understands; he is speaking mysteries by the Spirit.*
> — 1 CORINTHIANS 14:2 (NET)

People can also be baptized with the Holy Spirit and start speaking in tongues before they are baptized in water. Then it is important that they are baptized in water as soon as possible afterward.

What should I do next?

This was a little teaching on what a Christian is. If through this teaching, you have come to the realization that you do not know God and need forgiveness and to know Him, it can happen now. It is very simple. Today, you can be born again, as I was in April 1995. It is so amazing, and you will experience a supernatural life with God like we read about in the Bible. You can be forgiven today if you repent and turn to God:

> *The one who covers his transgressions will not prosper, but whoever confesses them and forsakes them will find mercy."*
> — PROVERBS 28:13 (NET)

Therefore, do not close your eyes and ears. God wants to forgive your sins and give you a whole new life. To receive His gift, you should do this: Turn away from your sins (repentance) and to God, and be baptized into Jesus Christ by full immersion in water.

Then you can receive the Holy Spirit and the new birth that the Bible talks about. You will not be judged for the things you have done wrong because they are all washed away.

What will you do with the forgiveness that Jesus offers to you?

Get in touch with us

Do you want to know more about how to be born again and live as a disciple of Jesus? We recommend you start reading the Book of Acts in the Bible. Here, you can read how the first disciples preached the gospel, healed the sick, and cast out demons, just like Christians do today. You can, as I have described here, read in the Book of Acts that everyone who came to faith was baptized right away. You can also read about how they received the Holy Spirit and began to speak in tongues.

We would also like to help you or put you in touch with someone near you who can help. Contact us, or others you know, who can baptize you into Jesus. Afterward, they can lay hands on you so you

lso are baptized with the Holy Spirit. You will
eceive eternal life and experience a living relation-
hip with God through Jesus Christ.

f you have questions, you can contact us through
ur website. Here, you can also watch some videos
howing what God is doing today.

Go to: **www.TheLastReformation.com**

You may also contact the person who gave you this
book:

_____

_____

_____

_____

My name:

_____

I repented and turned away from sins on this da

_____

I was baptized in water on this day:

_____

I was baptized with the Holy Spirit on this day:

_____

My precious memories:

_____

_____

_____

_____

_____